Grieving with Gratitude

Sisters from Different Misters

Iris J. Sarro, Ph.D.

Copyright © 2019 Iris J. Sarro, Ph.D.

All rights reserved. No part of this book may be used or reproduced by any means, graphic, electronic, or mechanical, including photocopying, recording, taping or by any information storage retrieval system without the written permission of the author except in the case of brief quotations embodied in critical articles and reviews.

This book is a work of non-fiction. Unless otherwise noted, the author and the publisher make no explicit guarantees as to the accuracy of the information contained in this book and in some cases, names of people and places have been altered to protect their privacy.

Balboa Press books may be ordered through booksellers or by contacting:

Balboa Press
A Division of Hay House
1663 Liberty Drive
Bloomington, IN 47403
www.balboapress.com
1 (877) 407-4847

Because of the dynamic nature of the Internet, any web addresses or links contained in this book may have changed since publication and may no longer be valid. The views expressed in this work are solely those of the author and do not necessarily reflect the views of the publisher, and the publisher hereby disclaims any responsibility for them.

The author of this book does not dispense medical advice or prescribe the use of any technique as a form of treatment for physical, emotional, or medical problems without the advice of a physician, either directly or indirectly. The intent of the author is only to offer information of a general nature to help you in your quest for emotional and spiritual well-being. In the event you use any of the information in this book for yourself, which is your constitutional right, the author and the publisher assume no responsibility for your actions.

Any people depicted in stock imagery provided by Getty Images are models, and such images are being used for illustrative purposes only.
Certain stock imagery © Getty Images.

Print information available on the last page.

ISBN: 978-1-9822-2726-5 (sc)
ISBN: 978-1-9822-2727-2 (hc)
ISBN: 978-1-9822-2734-0 (e)

Library of Congress Control Number: 2019906901

Balboa Press rev. date: 06/05/2019

To my husband who taught me that the material
things in this life are more temporal than we suspect
and the only thing that matters is to love and be loved

Contents

Introduction

My husband Christ had a phenomenal ability to start each day as a new day, as if he knew that every day we do things a little bit differently than we did the day before, in essence creating a new day every day even if we are in fact doing the same things. He seemed to know intuitively that our ability to adapt and flow with the process of life is a power within us even when we do not access it. This is the power that enables us to love ourselves, which becomes the basis for our ability to love others and to establish relationships based upon worth and value, something that will last and surround us in positive vibrations all our lives. Christ knew this intuitively, and he taught me this lesson over and over again. When I allowed the challenges in my life to stir up guilt, fear, criticism, and resentment toward myself that consequently impacted my relationships, he was there to help me stay in the moment and not fall prey to ruminating over yesterday or fearing tomorrow.

Unfortunately, a life can only be examined after it has been lived. When someone close to you dies, it shines a light on what is important. When my husband, Christ, passed away, it became clear that what was important to me was life's basics: love, family, and relationships. My reflections on the life told in this story are after the death of my husband. Søren Kierkegaard said, "Life can only be understood backwards; but it must be lived forwards." As I reflected on my sixty years with my husband, I began to really understand what we had lived.

In this book I recount the life of my husband and his friend whom he considered a brother. It is a story of friendship and the mortality we each face, and it is a testimonial to the adage "Yesterday is history, tomorrow is a mystery, and the present is a gift."

My husband had a gift for doing the right thing in any moment. He was happy and joyful most of his life. He lived by the words "Be kind and the rest will take care of itself." One of his favorite expressions was "Don't worry; nothing will be all right," followed by his unique laugh with a special meaning. People were often confused by his twist on the expression, but it was his way of saying that if you laugh at the things you're afraid of, the fear loses its power over you. If you're kind first and don't give in to fear, there is no need to worry about things coming out right. Sometimes the anxiety and fear embedded in worry are why things don't come out in the best interests of all concerned.

In my work as a school psychologist, I often saw that parents' and teachers' interactions with students were based more on worry than on kindness. Worries about success or achievement are based on concerns about yesterday or tomorrow. Parental or teacher actions based on such worries focus on the past or future and come from a place of fear. As such, they can lead to feelings of anxiety or fear for students. In comparison, actions based on concerns for the moment, without anxiety about the future or past, can come from kindness, not fear. Kindness, which is often overlooked in books about parenting and teaching, is best exemplified in the work of Fred Rogers. Fred Rogers, the creator and host of *Mister Rogers' Neighborhood*, which aired from 1968 to 2001, was the epitome of kindness. His program nurtured more than one generation of preschoolers, and he was instrumental in getting government funding for the Public Broadcasting Service (PBS), which provides high-quality programs that educate, enlighten, and enrich the public to help inform civil discourse essential to American society.

Perhaps being kind and living in the moment is the secret to a life well lived. The secret may be to live in the moment and to let life unfold rather than trying to make life experiences happen. My husband knew how to let go and let things unfold. I was fortunate to learn some lessons from my husband, but make no mistake, learning to let go and let things unfold is no easy lesson. I find now that he is gone I must continue to learn that lesson. When anxiety and fear prevent me from being able to adapt and flow with the process of life, I stop, listen, and try to hear his voice. It is times like these that I open my very old copy of Kahlil Gibran's *The Prophet*. In this book, long before he met me, Christ wrote an inscription to the woman that he would meet and spend his life with. The inscription reads, "Dearest, in this world where the material things are perhaps more temporal than we suspect, here is something that will last. With my love, Christ." Then I shed a tear, and thank Christ quietly for having been in my life.

Chapter 1

In the Beginning

In the beginning, a Canadian and an American meet at a university, establish a bond, and embark on a lifelong friendship, becoming brothers from different mothers. Each serves as best man in the other's wedding; each marries the love of his life. The two live in their respective countries, and they continue their journey, making memories in Canada and the United States while weaving the fabric of their lives.

There are voyages with children as extended families create memories that last a lifetime. These memories include birthdays in a summer cottage in Canada and winter visits to Florida. The fabric of their lives includes weddings of family and friends. There is a special wedding announcement on New Year's Eve. All these occasions create opportunities for the brothers to increase their bond and give their wives the opportunity to become sisters from different misters. Each brother gives the toast at the other's fiftieth wedding anniversary celebration. These events give each brother and his family the chance to reflect on the joy their friendship has brought. The sisters from different misters give each other support without hesitation when each loses the love of her life to that final destination.

This story of friendship and the mortality we each face is recounted here as a testimonial to the fact that yesterday is history, tomorrow is a mystery, and today is a gift. To ruminate over the past makes no sense, as it is gone. Nothing we do today will change the past, but we can learn from it. We cannot predict the future; consequently, it is a mystery. The choices made in the present will impact that future but will not necessarily determine it. Hence, what we do today can benefit from what we learned yesterday and what we hope for tomorrow. That is the gift of today. There is one thing that we know for certain about the future. We are born mortal and consequently we must die. There is no need to focus on death, as we know not when we will die. We know that it is the natural outcome of our mortality, and as such, we can enable it to dictate that we live our lives to the fullest every day.

There are many stories of impending mortality, such as *When Breath Becomes Air* by Paul Kalanithi, a talented neurosurgeon who was on the verge of a superlative medical career when he discovered he had stage IV cancer. He and his wife had many decisions to make and were forced to examine their values. He chose to share his story, writing with literary genius about his impending mortality. He made a poignant statement that has meaning for all of us: "Before my cancer was diagnosed, I knew that someday I would die, but I didn't know when. After the diagnosis, I knew that someday I would die, but I didn't know when." Death happens to all of us, regardless of our state of health. At the same time, we have to ask, If death is something that happens to all of us, what can we learn from it?

Another book recounting impending mortality is vice president Joe Biden's *Promise Me, Dad,* in which he recounts a year of hope, hardship, and purpose as his son Beau battled cancer. He speaks of how he and his family held fast to their family support system, focusing on Beau and each other through this difficult time. The family lived every day to the fullest, and Beau led the family in this resolve, saying, "All good. Let's do it. All good."

John McCain and his wife were interviewed on *60 Minutes.* He described the poor prognosis for his diagnosed brain cancer and said that he and his wife would do whatever they could to deal with the disease as best they could, but at the same time, they would "celebrate with gratitude a life well lived."

In the world of sports, we hear about athletic prowess associated with stories of mortality. In 2002, Joe Jurevicius cemented his place in NFL passing game history when he ran seventy-one yards on a pass in the NFC title game that resulted in the Buccaneers being Super Bowl–bound. At that time, Joe's newborn son was critically ill, and the boy passed away shortly thereafter. In a news article, Joe spoke of his experience grappling with his newborn son's mortality. He concluded that his son's life was cut short, but he described his son as a fighter. Joe described his connection to his newborn son, who he felt was running with him on that seventy-one-yard passing play.

What about the young fourteen-year-old athlete, Cailin with miraculous courage to live each day to the fullest? Despite a cancer diagnosis followed by surgery and chemo, she continued to pursue what she loved: competitive swimming. Her mother later recounted, after her daughter passed away, that water was Cailin's "happy place" and if she could move she was in the water. During multiple hospital stays, Cailin always focused on the important things in life, living in the moment. She was a fighter and inspired those in her world to have strength. Her last words to her mother were "I've got this, Mommy."

These stories are but a small sampling of the everyday human experience of grappling with death. The people in these stories were fighters, and they embodied the ability to light one little candle and bring out the best in themselves and those around them while remaining focused on living in the moment with the gift of the present.

Many people don't think of mortality unless they study philosophy, are met with a terminal diagnosis, or experience the actual passing of a loved one. Paul Kalanithi said it well in his literary gift to us, *When Breath Becomes Air*: "We know not when we will die, but our very birth engages us in a contract to die." Perhaps the real question we face, Kalanithi wrote, is not how long we live but rather how we want to live. We may not want to think about it, but that does not change the fact that we and our loved ones are going to die. From the moment we are born, each of us is facing our own mortality and the mortality of our loved ones. The newborn child—and everyone around the child—is joyous, as each should be. But that doesn't change the fact that birth is a beginning and death the destination.

At the age of twenty-one, I experienced the loss of my father and began a lifetime of lighting a memorial candle, a yahrzeit, to commemorate not only the death but also the spirit of my departed father. At the age of seventy-three, I added another yahrzeit to commemorate the spirit of my departed son, and at the age of seventy-eight,

I added yet another candle for my husband. I now light three memorial candles. I experience the joy and sadness of each of these significant others with a prayer for strength to understand that birth is a beginning, death a destination, and life a journey.

In order to experience a life well lived, we have to know what is most important to us. Our values help us determine who we want to be with, what we were put here to do, and how we want to spend our moments and days. To do this, we do not need to study philosophy or experience a tragedy. Nevertheless, we must live until we die—and to do that, we must make decisions. Our decisions are shaped by our values. How do we come to those values? We develop our values through our experiences, which may or may not be under our control. We also develop our awareness from within, from our personal perspectives.

Acknowledging our values and what is most important to us may become a priority if death is on the doorstep. Even if death is not on the doorstep, we would do well to become aware of our lives and how we are living them. Can we do that without defining our values or experiencing a terminal illness? If we can see how a life well lived unfolds, perhaps we can glean some insight into how we might experience it. Perhaps by sharing this story of how two brothers from different mothers experienced a life well lived, I may help others to reflect on their own lives. The sisters from different misters witnessed the joy and humor of the brothers from different mothers. The brothers shared this effortlessly with each other and all in their world. And it became a way of life for the sisters. In a way, it was a gift from the brothers, who taught the sisters how to live in the moment and experience the gift of the present.

Chapter 2

Life Choices

LIFE CHOICES, EVEN when seemingly simple, sometimes start a chain of events we least expect. One brother choses to leave Jamestown, his small, all-American hometown in upstate New York. He goes to the University of Illinois, one of the top ten universities in the Midwest, to study fine art. The other brother left his home in Toronto, Ontario, to go to the same university to study architecture.

At first glance, the American and the Canadian seemed to be different young men, but not really! Each was a first-generation, new-world child of immigrants who emigrated from Europe in search of a better life for themselves and their families. The Canadian's dad, John, came from a northeastern area of Poland under various Polish, Russian, and Ukrainian rulers. The American's dad, Pete, came from a northwestern area of Albania that was at various times under Turkish, Chinese, and Greek rule. These men from unstable European homelands were very appreciative of the opportunity to emigrate and become citizens of their new countries.

Both John and Pete married women from their same old-world background, and both held old-country family values. Each had a strong work ethic and each valued the opportunity given to him by his immigration to and citizenship in his new homeland. Their work ethic and values were reflected in their ability to start with nothing and accomplish much. Pete started in a low-level job in a furniture factory and worked his way up to vice president of the company. He was responsible for the stains used in each new furniture line. John started with nothing and built a frame shop of high quality. His children, Steve and Stella, expanded the frame shop and began designing high-end furniture. John's frame shop became Ruscana.

The brothers from different mothers brought their respective parents together at the Canadian's summer cottage in Lake of Bays, Ontario. The young men enjoyed showing off on the dock when not in the boat or the lake.

Summer at the cottage

The parents enjoyed being together and found many similarities between their lives. John and Pete each helped members of their old-world communities become established in the New World, creating an investment in family and friends. Perhaps this was the reason the brothers were intuitively invested in family and friends.

The brothers from different mothers shared many characteristics. Perhaps their parents' immigration to the New World to give their families a better life facilitated their talent for living in the present moment. They lived in the present and did so with humor and joy. They each had a phenomenal way of including others in their joyful antics. They both were excellent dancers. In essence, these were men, like their families with a love of life and a readiness to be a good neighbor to all who crossed their path. The brothers were a tribute to their families and a blessing to the families yet to come.

Chapter 3

Fraternity Days and Thereafter

RAISED IN THE households of first-generation immigrants, Steve, the Canadian, and Christ, the American, were ingrained with the concept that they had to be honorable so they would not bring disgrace to their families. Family values were an integral part of their existence and perhaps one that contributed to their bond.

They were honorable men who had respect for others, but as fraternity brothers, they engaged in many pranks that were just that. The pranks were honest fun and not intended to harm, but on occasion their pranks went too far, such as the time they hid all the silverware just before the fraternity was serving dinner to parents on parents' weekend. A few more pranks like that earned them the privilege of being kicked out of the fraternity house. They had to find somewhere else to live and ended up living with a philosophy professor. In the professor's home, their view of the world expanded, and their bond deepened.

Steve excelled in every sport except golf and basketball. Christ was a natural athlete who maintained the record for the most three-point shots on the Jamestown High School varsity basketball team. In addition, Christ caddied for members of Moonbrook Country Club, one of whom gave him a set of golf clubs. Christ shot a score of eighty-five his first time out and loved the challenge of improving his game.

At some point, Christ joined Steve at the cottage in Lake of Bays. Steve's sister, Stella, booked Christ to play in a tournament at the Bracebridge Golf Club. Christ had a large gallery of fans and won second place. Steve and Stella wanted him to win. When Stella asked him why he didn't win, Christ responded, "It is not polite to go to someone else's club and beat the club champ." When Christ and Steve played golf at the Bigwin Island Resort in Lake of Bays, Steve lost seventeen balls. Needless to say, after that, the brothers enjoyed each other's company in many places but not on the golf course.

After their junior year in college, the American was drafted into the army, and the Canadian left the university to attend the Frank Lloyd Wright school in Arizona.

Christ at Fort George G. Meade

The brothers stayed in touch with one another. When Christ's brother, Tom, married in Jamestown, Steve and his parents were invited to the wedding. By then Steve had met his future wife, Betty, and Christ had met me. Betty and I met at Tom's wedding. She and I were comfortable with each other, and the four of us enjoyed our weekend in Jamestown.

When Christ and I got married, Christ did not hesitate to ask Steve to be his best man, and Steve was delighted. It was a small wedding held at the university, and consequently there were many telegrams from family and friends unable to make the trip to the Midwest. As best man, Steve had the responsibility of reading these telegrams. The only issue was that many of the telegrams from Christ's family were written in Albanian. Steve rose to the occasion, reading the telegrams with some help, and then danced the Greek *valle* while shouting "Opa!"

Christ's wedding—"Opa!"

Christ and I went to Toronto for our honeymoon, and at Steve's invitation, we went up to his cottage. We were alone in the small cottage by the lake at first, and then Steve, Betty, and Stella joined us. They shared stories of previous visits to the cottage, like when Christ joined Steve and Stella at the Bigwin Resort to dance to the music of the big bands. Even though the era of the Big Bands was over, I was indoctrinated into the cottage culture of Lake of Bays, Ontario, and loved it!! During our honeymoon, Stella arranged for Christ to play golf. He shot a seventy-three for eighteen holes at the Mississaugua Golf and Country Club, a historic club where golf legends have played. I became convinced that Christ had enough energy for it all: golf, dancing, and honeymooning.

Two weeks after our honeymoon, Christ played in the Illinois State Amateur Golf Tournament at the Savoy Golf Club at the University of Illinois. I caddied for him barefoot. The president of the Illinois State Amateur Golf Association suggested that Christ get a "real caddy." Christ replied that he had his caddy. Christ was runner-up in a sudden-death playoff. He lost to a five-time winner who had won for the first time when Christ was two years old. The local newspaper ran articles on Christ, describing him as "the hometown boy who was no Beau Brummell, but [who] could sure play golf."

Golf, golf, and more golf!

Christ was best man in Steve's wedding the following year. In spite of the formal attire of the wedding party, the boys engaged in their usual fun and love of life, drawing all those around them into the joy. The brothers had enriched their personal lives with their marriages, and their careers had expanded as well. Steve had an eye for good design and applied that to the manufacture of furniture. He and his sister, Stella, added their talents to those of their father in the pursuit of fine furniture at Ruscana in Toronto, Canada. Christ worked for the government as an illustrator in the Pentagon. He was a fine artist, and one of his etchings, The Alleyway, was hung in the Corcoran Gallery of Art in Washington, DC.

The alleyway

In addition to expanding his career as a fine artist, he continued to enjoy golf and improve his game, playing in many amateur golf tournaments. In order to further pursue his talent for golf, Christ leveraged his talent as a graphic artist in government service to get a position running the graphic branch of Central Command. This job took him to MacDill Air Force Base in Tampa, Florida.

Betty and I shared with each other our stories of meeting the loves of our lives. I told her of my first date with Christ. He had returned to the university after being drafted and was living alone in a studio apartment. He did not know anyone, but he met a girl at a rally. He called her to go out for a cup of coffee. The girl, who lived on my dorm floor, was busy and could not go. She ran down the hall to tell me she had a New Yorker on the phone and asked me if I wanted to go out with him for coffee. I was a seventeen-year-old freshman. I had lived in New York and Miami Beach before coming to the university and was a bit homesick for New York. I took the phone call and agreed to go out for coffee. I wasn't taking any chances, though. I waited downstairs for the blind date so I could scope him out first.

When a man walked in with a London Fog raincoat and a pipe in his mouth, I decided I would go out with him whether he was the blind date or not. I walked over to the water fountain near the house phone so I could hear who he asked for. Being a leg man, he eyed my legs as I took a drink of water at the fountain. Luckily, he asked for Iris on the phone, and I turned around and said, "I'm Iris."

During the coffee date, Christ bragged about his prowess on the dance floor and his artistic talent. When we returned to my dormitory, I put on a Harry Belafonte record, and sure enough, this man could dance. The next day he returned with a sketch of Kelly, the famous circus clown. He'd drawn it on a shirt cardboard from a folded shirt because he did not have a canvas. The drawing wasn't very impressive to me, and I said I didn't think Christ was much of an artist. Christ went away, worked on it all night, and brought it back the next day with a finished portrait of Kelly. The rendition of Kelly was phenomenal. The rest is history. Many people have offered thousands to buy *Kelly the Clown*, which is not for sale. It still hangs in my home to this day as a reminder of the beginning of a love story.

Kelly the Clown

Betty told me of when she first saw Steve. Steve came by boat from his family cottage to the resort store where seventeen-year-old Betty was working as one of two postmistresses during the summer cottage season. When she first saw him, she immediately was aware of his presence. He had his German shepherd with him and was wearing a striped muscle shirt and tight black calypso pants covered with a poncho from his Frank Lloyd Wright days. She was instantly drawn to him. He kept coming back to the store for more milk than his family could possibly use at the cottage. Betty got to the point where she recognized the sound of his boat motor and would run down the hill to wait on him even if she wasn't on duty.

That summer Steve had a bet with his brother from another mother that he would shave his head. Needless to say, these fun-loving boys would stop at nothing, and Steve shaved his head. He went from looking like Kirk Douglas to a lumpy Yul Brynner. Unfortunately, Christ never paid the bet, but fortunately, the bald head was a factor in Steve and Betty's soon-to-be love affair. Betty went to town and bought a white sailor gob hat to cover

Steve's head. Although his wonderful head of hair grew back, he wore a white gob hat the rest of his life.

Little did Betty and I know that over the years, as our husbands' bond grew and our families shared many memorable moments, we would become sisters from different misters. We quickly learned that the brothers had a gentle, serious side coupled with their fun-loving joy of living. On one trip to Toronto the brothers were celebrating their birthdays, which were just two days apart. Of course there was a birthday cake and a trip to the store at the bay. Steve had a wardrobe of cashmere vests and was often replenishing them. The boys always enjoyed each other's company, regardless of what they were doing. They were usually helpful to their wives, but hanging clothes was a bit more than either would do, unless they were with the other goofing around.

Birthdays in Canada

Shopping for argyle vests at the bay

Hanging clothes—really?

Visits to Canada revealed even more of their multifaceted joy of living. One time Christ had to bring a toilet seat cover from the US because Steve couldn't get it in Canada. Bringing the toilet seat over the border was nothing compared to the shenanigans of installing it. Each trip included a visit to the cottage, and without fail there was the usual goofing-off, good-natured fun. When the boys went off to run errands, it was guaranteed that they would have a good time and share joy with others, but there was no telling how they would come back. One time they came back with tattoos!

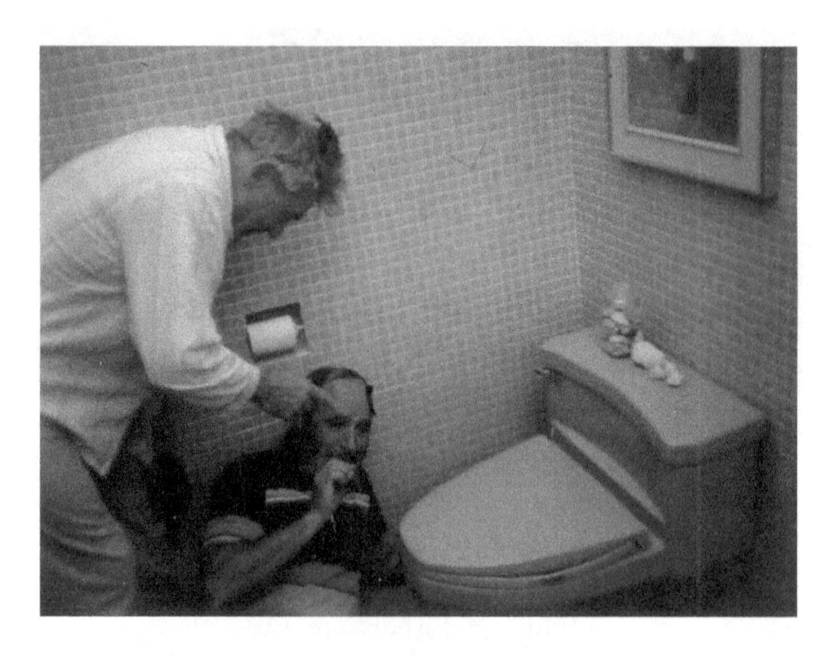

Installing a toilet lid brought in from the US

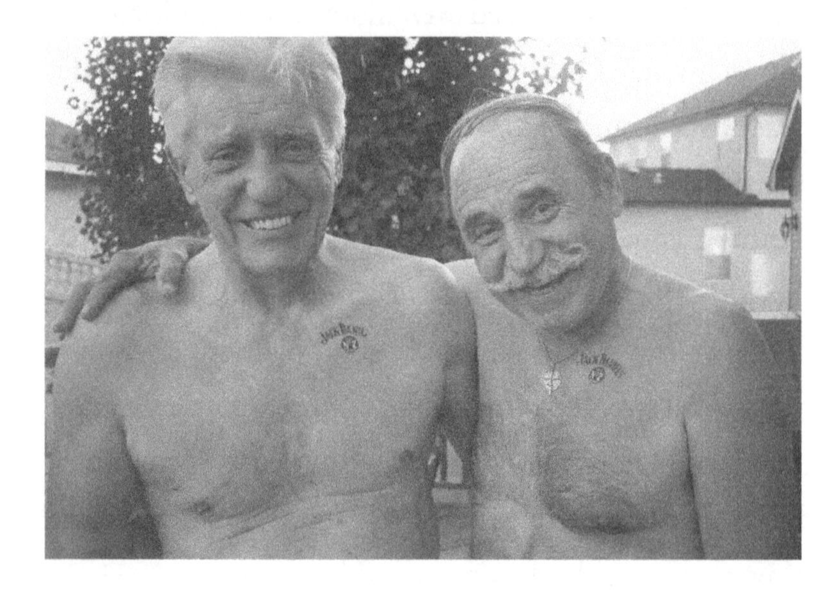

Tattoos—really!

Discussing politics in Jamestown

With the brothers' laughter and joy of living, their family and friends, especially the older generation, always welcomed their visits to Jamestown. On our many trips to Jamestown the brothers would meet and in between laughter and joy would discuss politics from their Canadian and American perspectives.

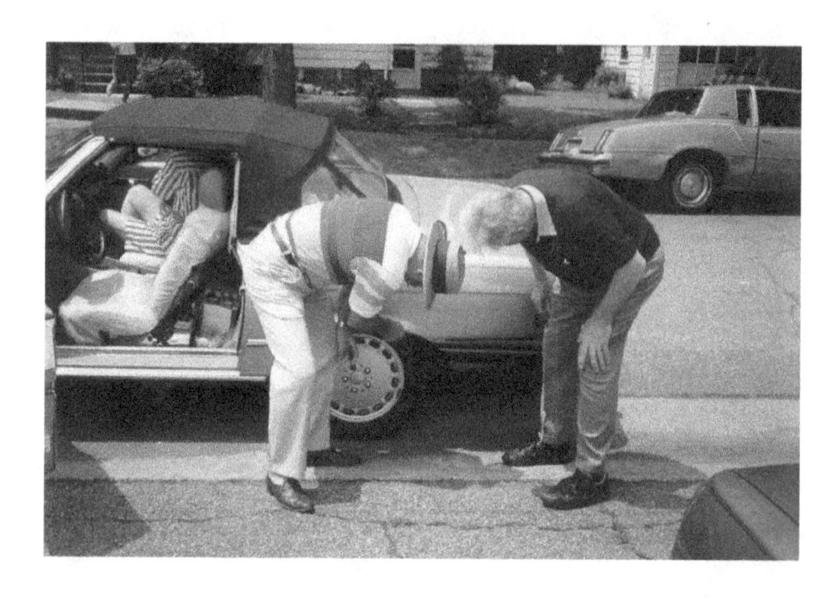

Preparing to leave Jamestown

Chapter 4

The Dogs: Butch, Blitzkreig, Blitz Ezeze & Mjeker i thinjur Butchie, & Jacques Cousteau

THE DOGS WERE an integral part of the many trips to Canada and Florida. First, there was the Canadian dog Butch. Then the American dog Blitzkreig. Followed by the Canadian dog Blitzkrieg called "Blitz". Then the American poodles Ezeze and Mjeker i thinjur. Then the American dog Butch called "Butchie". And then finally the last dog, a Bichon Frise, Jacques Cousteau.

Both Steve and Christ had a love affair with German shepherds. First there was Butch, Steve's family's German shepherd. Christ fell in love with Butch. When Christ visited his friend in Canada his love for Butch increased. Consequently, the American longed for his own German shepherd.

Knowing I was not a dog aficionado, Christ and our school-age children surprised me with a shepherd puppy they'd bought in Florida. I could not disappoint them, so the puppy took up residence. My only choice in the matter was choosing a name for this new family member. I'm Jewish, and since the puppy's arrival was a surprise attack on me, we named him Blitzkrieg—Blitz for short—after the intense military campaign designed to bring about a swift victory. Obviously Christ and the children's surprise attack was intended to get a shepherd dog at all costs. Mission accomplished! But Blitz did not have any formal training and was an unruly dog.

When Pete, Christ's father, was widowed, he came to live with us, which delighted his grandchildren. After Blitz, a black miniature poodle took up residence in our household. Grandpa named the dog Ezeze, which translates to "Blackie" in Albanian. Christ decided to breed Ezeze. After the deed was done, it was apparent that Ezeze would have her litter at the time of a long-awaited family trip to Toronto for the two families to be together. We took the trip anyway, driving from Tampa to Toronto. Our two school-age children could not fight with each other in the back seat because they were separated by a box that held Ezeze and her one-week-old puppies. Ezeze's pups were wonderful. In due time they went to brighten a number of other households, but we kept the runt. Christ's father gave the pup the Albanian name Mjeker i thinjur, which translates to "Gray Beard."

The Canadian visit was a hit as always. Steve did not have a dog at the time, and all the children enjoyed playing with the puppies. Meanwhile, the brothers from different mothers engaged in their joyful antics. Steve and Christ were masters at having fun, and Christ's infectious laugh drew everyone into their escapades. They managed to find the small experiences of everyday life amusing, like the time they discovered they were both missing the same tooth.

Missing the same tooth

Butch had gone to dog heaven on his final journey. Steve and Betty got a wonderful shepherd and named him "Blitzkreig von Kinder Freund" in honor of Blitz, who was in heaven with the Canadian Butch and von Kinder Freund which translates to "Friend of Children." The American family continued their summer trips, enjoying the family outings and the banter of the brothers.

Discussing politics in Canada

Years later, when we no longer had the poodles Ezeze and Mjeker i thinjur, Christ and I went to Toronto for New Year's Eve to help our friends enjoy the surprise announcement of Stella's marriage. There were more flight attendants than passengers on that flight because everyone else was flying to Florida. Steve and Betty met us at the airport with down coats and boots.

The brothers at Stella's announcement party

On New Year's Day, Christ was sitting in Steve's kitchen petting Blitz and asked Steve to call Blitz's breeder. The brothers began their usual joyful banter, with the Canadian saying that the breeder would not have a litter at this time of the year. They went back and forth, Christ insisting that Steve call the breeder and Steve insisting the breeder would have no pups. Finally, to end the fiasco, a call was made to the breeder, who had one pup left from an unexpected litter.

Typical bantering brothers

The American bought the pup sight unseen and decided on Butchie for his name, after the Canadian's original shepherd. Christ turned to me and refused to take no for an answer. He told me that he would pay for the dog with a gold piece he had won in a golf tournament. I agreed on the condition that Christ promise to hire a trainer to be sure Butchie would be a well-mannered dog.

The breeder would not allow the shepherd pups to be released until they were nine weeks old. The Canadian's son Andrew, who was in college, volunteered to bring the pup to Florida on spring break. Butchie won the hearts of the Canadian family, and Andrew did not want to let the puppy go to his home in Florida. Unfortunately, Andrew did not come to Florida on spring break, so Butchie had to be flown to Florida in a crate. Christ went to the airport long before the arrival time to wait. Soon Butchie was on Florida soil, and Christ's dream of having his own Canadian-bred German shepherd was fulfilled

Christ with puppy Butchie in Florida

I developed serious low-back problems after planting a crape myrtle tree. The American doctors identified the pain as a function of spinal stenosis, slippage at the L4 and L5 with lumbar degenerative disc disease. They recommended treatment interventions that were unsuccessful and ultimately recommended surgery, but each of the doctors recommended a different surgical intervention dependent upon their respective disciplines of neurology or orthopedics. I was dependent on pain medication but did not want surgery since there was no consensus.

After researching the work of Dr. Hamilton Hall, a back doctor in Canada, I called for an appointment. Dr. Hall was closing his practice and preparing to spend his time promoting his work and training doctors, but as fate would have it, he granted me a consultation. Christ and I went to visit our friends in Toronto so I could see Dr. Hall at a Canadian hospital. Dr. Hall agreed with the structural diagnosis of his American counterparts, but he said that in Canada they did not operate on disc disease. With the help of the Canadian Back Institute, I began my journey of recovery. Then a phone consult with Caroline Myss, who was just beginning her journey as a medical clairvoyant, led to a decision to not have surgery.

With another stroke of positive vibrations, I went to a pain management clinic in Springfield, Missouri, that was part of a National Institutes of Health (NIH) research project addressing the widespread use of pain medication. As part of this project, the clinic offered an alternative program designed to get patients off pain medication and using more natural healing in the form of meditation. Christ and I returned from Springfield with renewed hope of healing for my back and a new putter for Christ's golf club arsenal.

Positive vibrations continued in our world as I met the man who had developed music beds for the Springfield project. He lived not far from Christ and me. He made a music chair for me, and I continued to use the vibrations of music to reduce my pain. I found a Feldenkrais teacher, and the process of healing continued. The process was slow. Butchie was at my side throughout the ordeal, and together we stretched and meditated as the healing continued. I became a dog aficionado, and Butchie became adept at meditation. During meditation he was known to collapse in total relaxation on his side.

One year the University of Illinois played a postseason game at the Citrus Bowl in Orlando, and it was as good an excuse as any for the brothers and their families to visit. Since the Canadians needed to put their Blitz down, they were happy to visit and be with Butchie, who was a wonderful dog. Butchie brought much joy to Christ and me as well as our family, which by now included grandchildren: Taylor, Morgan, Kyra, and Connor. As a special note, we had a family tradition of calling family members on their birthday, and Butchie would harmonize at the end of the birthday song in person or on the phone. We had always intended to record Butchie's howling in perfect unison with the end of the Happy Birthday song, but we never did.

Butchie singing happy birthday

University of Illinois at the Citrus Bowl

The brothers with Butchie in Florida

Christ and I planned a trip to Scotland to allow me to present at the International School Psychology Association conference held at the University of Dundee. At first Christ, who was retired, was annoyed saying I worked too much, but then Christ realized the University was in Scotland and a twenty-minute car ride to St. Andrews. He immediately said, "You go write while I pack!" I secured a tee time for us with Golf Pac since it would otherwise require that we take a chance on a lottery and not be able to play. It was Christ's opportunity to follow in the footsteps of golf legends at the oldest and most iconic golf course in the world, the place where golf began. Since Christ was a scratch golfer, a visit to the place where golf began was a pilgrimage.

We planned to visit Steve and Betty before going to Scotland so we could leave Butchie with them while we were away. Their Blitz was gone, and they were happy to have Butchie. The Canadians were selling their home in Toronto and planning a move to Calgary, where their youngest son, Chris, was living with his wife, Bree. As life unfolds, the house was sold just before we arrived. Christ and I helped them pack up their house for the move.

The Canadians were planning to rent a condo temporarily before moving to Calgary. The condo only allowed pets for the owner, not for renters. So I arranged for Butchie to stay at a kennel while we were in Scotland. After we left on our trip, at the last minute, Steve and Betty could not bear for Butchie to go to a kennel, which he had never done before. Consequently, they smuggled Butchie into the condo rental. Butchie stayed with his surrogate family and had his first experience leaving his parents, going up and down stairs, and riding in an elevator. And if that was not enough, when Christ and I returned from Scotland, we joined Steve and Betty at their cottage, and Butchie had his first experience swimming in a Canadian lake. Summertime at the cottage was a perfect time to celebrate Betty's and my birthdays, which were only a week apart.

After our trip to Scotland and Canada we returned home. We had many more good years with Butchie who bought joy to the children in my private practice as a school psychologist. At the age of 12 1/2 when Butchie's quality of life was seriously compromised, my husband made the difficult decision to let go of Butchie. Our son Kevin was with us. Butchie's veterinarian from birth returned his ashes to us in a beautiful urn with a copy of the rainbow bridge prose that depicts your pet waiting to greet you when you reach the destination on your journey.

For the next seven years with an empty nest and without a dog we enjoyed an easy lifestyle which included travel. Although we missed Butchie we never intended to get another dog. Then when least expected another dog came into our lives. Valentine, my friend of many years, had always wanted a Bichon Frise and found a litter. She asked if I wanted to go with her to pick out her puppy and be the "god mother" for her new dog. When I discovered the litter was at a home on the cul de sac where Christ and I lived, I called my husband to tell him that the neighbor dog we saw every day was not overweight, but was pregnant and had a litter. My husband joined Valentine and me at the neighbor's house and when the tiny, white, fluffy puppies tumbled out of the bedroom into the family room where we were waiting, we were all in awe. One little cotton ball with a black nose and black eyes kept going up to Christ even though Christ pushed him away several times. The next thing I knew I was not only a god mother to Valentine's Hemsley, but a mother to Helmsley's litter mate. The new puppy needed a name and since he was a French breed, we needed a French name and in a moment Helmsley's litter mate was named Jacques Cousteau.

Jacques Cousteau

Chapter 5

Glad Times, Sad Times

Betty and I shared many moments in Toronto, Tampa, Jamestown, and the Lake of Bays. When we were not together, we were experiencing the trials and tribulations of raising a family and engaging in the many active sports of our children, including competitive skiing for the Canadians and competitive swimming for the Americans. We each experienced respectively the gamut of life experiences—providing support for our husbands, surviving the passing of parents and in-laws, celebrating our children's graduations and marriages, and rejoicing in the arrival of grandchildren.

Steve and Betty moved to Calgary from Toronto and eventually moved in with Chris, their youngest son, and his family. Christ and I went to the Calgary Stampede, dressing in appropriate western gear. The Stampede was never quite the same again after the invasion of the brothers from different mothers. Lunch at a restaurant brought out the usual antics of the brothers.

Brothers at the Calgary stampede

Betty and Iris at Calgary Stampede

Christ during the Stampede

The four of us were ready to watch the chuck wagon races, and as a good friend, I asked them to announce Betty's birthday on the jumbotron, which boasted a very large screen and was coupled with the public address system. Unfortunately, they announced her age as seventy when she was only sixty. Somehow I was held responsible for the incorrect age when all I did was ask them to announce my friend's birthday. Days later, at a celebration dinner for my birthday, somehow I ended up with pie in my face. It seemed the joyful antics of the brothers had become a part of us sisters' moments in life.

Birthday LunchPie in the Face

Christ and I continued dancing our hearts away at our country club. Christ started a Greek Open golf tournament at the club. A rival golf club retaliated with an Italian Open, and Christ won the championship fight. George Zaharias presented the prize, which included the putter of Babe Zaharias, an Olympic athlete who, in 1934, was the first female golfer to enter the all-male PGA tournament, an event not duplicated again until sixty-eight years later. The putter will eventually be donated to the Babe Zaharias public links golf club started by the Babe in Tampa.

The rhythm of life continued with many happy times, but the sad times could not be avoided. After twelve years of joy and purpose, Butchie had to take his final journey to dog heaven. The Canadians came to visit, and the brothers took a moment to hold Butchie's urn and share how much joy their dogs had brought into their lives. Life must go on, and the four of us visited a park in Florida where the brothers became buddies with a gorilla.

Celebrating Butchie's life

Becoming buddies with a gorilla

Christ and I, who continued to reside in Tampa, planned a trip to Calgary to visit our Canadian friends. That 2004 trip was a perfect example of sad and glad times, two sides to a coin. The trip happened to coincide with the Stanley Cup hockey excitement. The Eastern Conference champions, the Tampa Bay Lightning, defeated the Western Conference champions, the Calgary Flames, in a seven-game series and were awarded the Stanley Cup. It was Tampa Bay's first ever appearance in the final. It was the Calgary Flames' third appearance and the first since their championship season of 1989. The brothers from different mothers engaged in their typical antics, with the Canadian wearing a Tampa Bay Lightning hat with a frown and his thumb pointed down and the American wearing a Calgary Flames shirt with a smile and thumb up.

Stanley Cup, Tampa beats Calgary

There were more trips and more memories to be made. Our children were grown but living nearby. When Steve and Betty came to Florida, they saw our kids and grandkids, and when Christ and I went to Canada, we saw their kids and grandkids. The brothers' bond continued and they continued discussing politics, but this time with input from Christ's new dog, Jacques Cousteau.

Discussing politics, with Jacques Cousteau

Glad times continued with the Canadians' trip to Florida in October to celebrate the brothers' birthdays. My daughter-in-law, Steph, prepared a homemade cake for the brothers that was a much-appreciated birthday gift. The brothers each had a sweet tooth. Steve, Betty,

Christ, and I made a trip to the Disney park to see our favorite characters.

Birthday cake in Florida

Birthday trip to Disney

The brothers from different mothers celebrated their respective fiftieth wedding anniversaries together. Steve and Betty joined Christ and me with family and friends on a cruise to the Bahamas. Steve was relieved that there were no telegrams in Albanian to read. The brothers were delighted to dance again at the anniversary celebration, shouting "Opa!" in typical Greek style. The following year Christ and I joined Steve and Betty with their family and friends in Banff at the spot where Steve proposed to Betty. Then the families celebrated lunch outdoors in a lovely venue. At each fiftieth anniversary celebration, the best man gave yet another toast to the bride and groom, only this time in the presence of kids and grandkids. The differences in these toasts fifty years later reflected their wealth of wonderful moments shared over the years.

50th Wedding AnniversaryToast

Opa!! Again 50 years later

Goofing off as usual

Chris's wife, Bree, made a battery-operated anniversary clock for Betty and Steve. The clock has their wedding picture at twelve o'clock, a picture of their fiftieth anniversary at six o'clock, and a picture of them kissing at nine o'clock. Around the outside of the clock are the words "All you need for a happy marriage is a good sense of humor and a poor memory."

In 2010 Betty was with Steve when he passed away. We were sad at the passing of our friend but glad that we had gone to Calgary to celebrate New Years Eve with them several months before. Christ and I went to the celebration of Steve's life to be with Betty and the family and friends.

As fate would have it, Chris and Bree brought their three children to Orlando for a winter trip. We visited them in Orlando and then Chris and his family made a trip to Tampa to have a glorious lunch with Kevin and his family. Two months later, in February, Kevin, at the age of forty-eight, suddenly made his final journey to heaven. Ironically, Kevin died on the same day that my father, who never met his grandson, died. Betty, who had not planned to come to Florida that winter, came from Calgary and stayed a while to support her husband's brother from another mother and her sister from a different mister. Her son Stephen came from Toronto as well, and every year thereafter Stephen called Christ to wish him a happy Father's Day, because Stephen did not have his father and Christ did not have his son.

When the family returned from the celebration of Kevin's life, Christ and I found a monarch butterfly on the walkway to our home. It is said that butterflies embody the spirit of the human soul. Betty believes if you tell a butterfly "I love you," it will fly to heaven to deliver your message. Christ kept the butterfly on his drafting table. From an unknown author are the following words:

> A gentle reminder that we are never far apart
>
> My spirit will live on forever, there within your heart
>
> And when you see a butterfly here to brighten your day
>
> Remember I am there with you, and there I'll always stay

For five years, Betty came every February to be with Christ and me. Then the next winter, because of pressing concerns in Calgary, she did not come. That year in February, we were with our daughter in our favorite brunch place when Christ collapsed at Breakfast.

The last words our daughter said to him were "I love you." It is said that hearing is the last of the five senses to be lost by one passing into the next realm. Someone called 911. The first responder to arrive was a sheriff, followed by an ambulance, which took Christ to the emergency room (ER). When the ER doctor came to tell me that they could not restart Christ's heart, my greatest fear was realized. The realization set in that it was time for my husband to continue on his journey without me. It is said that when your work on this earth is done, it is time for the spirit to go on to the next chapter. It is also said that people will not go on to the next leg of their journey until they are sure their loved ones who remain behind will be okay. For those who remain behind, it may not be the time that they would choose to let go of their loved one. If their loved one must go, we must be respectful of it and learn our own lesson of letting go. Hospital staff was kind in allowing me as much time as I needed with my husband to tell him I loved him before the family joined us in the quiet room.

Although Betty had not planned to come to Florida that winter, once she heard the news, she was on a plane to Tampa. My sister from a different mister was again there to ease the pain as my family went through the loss of Christ. Kevin's oldest daughter, Taylor, created a shadow box of memorabilia of her grandfather's life. She included the butterfly Christ found after Kevin's celebration of life. Kevin's youngest daughter, Morgan, came from college to be with the family. Our other grandchildren, Kyra and Connor, and their spouses came from their out-of-town homes. Christ was interred at the Florida National Cemetery in Bushnell. Christ's ashes were placed in the scatter garden with azalea bushes. Butterflies appeared above the flowers and I said "I love you" so the butterflies could deliver the message to Christ. We said The Lord's Prayer with my nephew Peter reciting it in Greek and me reciting it in English.

Tree above azalea bushes

Betty and I were blessed to be with our husbands when they each went on to their next adventure. I know in my heart that the brothers stayed as long as they could and departed only when they were sure that the love of their life would be okay. If we exist in spirit form before we take physical form, then at death, when the physical form can no longer support the spirit, it is released. If two spirits are entwined in love, perhaps the spirit of the survivor joins the spirit of the deceased when it is time for that reunion.

Betty and I know the love of the brothers is still with us. We have each experienced signs from our loved ones. Christ and I were with Betty and her family at Steve's celebration of life. During the celebration, Steve's oldest granddaughter, Alex, got a call on her cell phone. It was a gravelly man's voice that said, "How is the rowing?" Steve had encouraged his granddaughter to row in high school, as it was a sport he had loved. A month later Betty realized the anniversary clock that, Bree, made had stopped at precisely the time Steve passed away.

After the celebration of life for Christ, Betty and I were with family and friends in front of our villa. Christ's and I owned a townhome on the golf course. A golf ball ricocheted off the roof of the house and landed in front of the gathering. It was not an impossible event, but it was a highly improbable one and one that had never occurred before. Our villa was at the end of a row of town houses parallel to the fairway. For a shot to ricochet off the roof, it would have needed to be a well-hit drive coupled with a drastic hook. The group agreed that it was a sign from Christ that I would get some much-needed help from above when I played golf.

Another sign came from Christ's favorite bird clock. The clock chime on the hour in the form of different bird sounds was something Christ loved. Unfortunately it had always annoyed me. So when the battery died, we never replaced it. Though the clock had been stopped for several years, it had stopped at the exact time Christ passed away. I did not notice where the hands were on the clock until weeks after Christ's heart stopped. Some people would explain Betty's clock and my clock as coincidence, but Betty and I feel otherwise.

It is said that the angels cry when someone precious is taken from a loved one left on earth. When Christ passed away, the pond behind our house was dry from a drought. After his funeral, there was an unseasonal downpour, and the pond filled up. Perhaps it was a coincidence, or maybe it is possible that the angels do cry when they want to tell someone left on earth that they are sending their love from above.

Betty and I continue to celebrate life's moments as we move into new experiences with our children and grandchildren. We share many moments with each other's families, spending time in the US or Canada. Our families are truly an extension of each other.

Life goes on. During a trip to Canada, Betty congratulated my grandson on his engagement, and I congratulated Betty's granddaughter Alex on her engagement. Stella, sharing in the moment via phone, said, "No pressure on setting dates for the weddings. Just make sure they do it before we die." Stella got her wish, my grandson Connor got married, and he and his wife, Kendyl, have a beautiful baby girl named Elle. So Betty was able to welcome my first great-grandchild into the world. Stella got her wish, and we all danced at Alex's wedding. In addition, Taylor and her fiancé, Matt, announced their engagement, and yet another granddaughter's wedding is on the horizon. Perhaps Betty and I will be blessed to enjoy Morgan's continuing travel adventures, the joys of Kyra and Peter's union, and the ultimate adventures of Chris's children, Zack, Avery, and Nolan.

One thing is certain: life will hold more glad and sad times, and the sisters from different misters will continue to celebrate moments together and experience the joys of aging. Even though they are now, for a little while, alone, without the brothers from different mothers who brought them together, perhaps they will rejoin the loves of their life in spirit when it is time for them to journey on to their final destination.

Brothers from different mothers

Chapter 6

Holding On or Letting Go

Losing a loved one can be a roller-coaster ride that forces us to hold on or let go while hoping to survive the experience. After the sudden death of the love of my life, I realized that the many lessons Christ taught me did not end with his death. In fact, he continued to teach me the most valuable lesson of all: being present in the moment. It was something he did intuitively and something I had unknowingly been learning since I met him.

I discovered, like many who have lost a partner, that every first without your loved one is difficult. There's the first holiday you celebrate alone—maybe it's Thanksgiving or Christmas or Passover. And there's every other first, like the first time you go to your favorite restaurant, watch your favorite show, or go anywhere new that your partner would have loved. The sadness is overwhelming! Knowing that you will never get over the loss, but must go on is so difficult. K. Heitzmann, in her book Unforgotten states "Grief is a coat you put on and off wearing it only until it has warmed the chill of loss, but not so long as to take the edge from memory." As a way to work through my grief, I began to journal my thoughts and feelings.

Betty stayed weeks on end after the funeral to help me get through the sadness. Betty had been widowed years earlier, and her presence and my journaling evolved into what became *Sisters from Different Misters.*

The summer after Christ passed away, I went to Canada to be with Betty. We shared our birthdays once again and spent time with Andrew and his wife, Wanda, at their new home. Andrew, Betty, and Stella helped me with the chronology of the many trips back and forth to America and Canada. It was a time of laughter and tears and included a new memory in Andrew's home. A severe storm left Betty, Stella, and me stranded in the dark and Wanda and Andrew unable to get home because of huge trees down on their access road. While there was severe damage to neighboring homes, the damage and electrical outage at Andrew's place was minor in comparison.

On this trip, Andrew took Wanda, Stella, Betty, and me on a boat trip on Lake of Bays to visit with old friends who still had their cottage next door to Steve's original cottage. Although it had been almost sixty years since Christ and I stayed at the cottage on our honeymoon and the cottage had since changed hands, the small cabin at the water's edge was still there. Looking at the honeymoon cottage which was unchanged, I experienced the sadness of Christ not being here with me in that moment. Then I realized that somehow he *was* with me. At times like this, Christ's absence is a sadness that overtakes me, but at the same time, I feel glad and grateful that he was in my life. I could not describe this mixed emotion for a long time, until I discovered the term *happy sorrow.* The feeling is a sense that the moment doesn't have to be sad; it just has to be different.

Flowers can live on after they die if the memory of their beauty and scent live on in the heart and mind of someone who was blessed to have them in his or her life. In the same way that the beauty of a flower can live on, the spirits of loved ones live on in the hearts of those who loved them. My granddaughter Taylor once said that when you find someone who can make you laugh, smile, grow, lust, want, crave, feel, and make you mad but happy, keep that. That's euphoria. In the circle of life, the spirit of a person whom you love and who has loved you does not disappear.

Through all of this, I learned that all life ends with a purpose and the legacy left behind. If the greatest gift is to love and be loved, then loved ones do not die as long as the living hold on to their spirits in a meaningful way. Perhaps this is the meaning of the Greek expression *Eonia Ei Mnimi*—everlasting be your memory.

Author's Note

Telling the story has enriched my life and hopefully will enrich the lives of its readers.

I have written school psychological reports to assist the student, teachers, and parents to maximize the student's response to life challenges in and out of school. The greatest learning experience is not in school, but in all life experiences. I always knew I would write a book, but I did not know what it would be until that moment after leaving the jewelry store. In that moment, I was informed what I was going to write about and how I was going to write it. In that moment, I came to understand what Søren Kierkegaard meant when he said, "Life can only be understood backwards; but it must be lived forwards."

The meaning of the saying "Birth is a beginning, death a destination, and life a journey" also became clear as I journaled my thoughts for this book. It is clear to me now that what I have always suspected is true: life is the greatest classroom for learning. Learning is nothing more than a change in behavior. With each life experience, we may learn or not. We may change our behavior or repeat the previous behavior. We may not be able to control the extent to which our lives take us from birth to adulthood to old age, but we are in control of how we respond to moments. The moments in our past, present, and future are a culmination of our learning—the changes in behavior that take us each step of the way from one stage to the next as we move along our journey from birth to our destination. Life is truly a journey, with birth the beginning and death the destination. We go step by step from the beginning to the destination in the greatest classroom for learning that exists.

We can think of this journey from birth to eventual death in secular terms. We are born, we work, we live, and we die. Or we might chose to think of this journey in spiritual terms, seeing the stage-by-stage journey from the beginning, birth, to the destination, death, as a sacred pilgrimage to life everlasting. The individual's choice of secular or spiritual explanation is undoubtedly a result of the learning that has occurred in his or her life journey. Nevertheless, the journey is made in the greatest classroom with experiences that shape who we are and the legacy we leave to those whom we have loved and who have loved us.

Author with Christ and his dog Jacques Cousteau

About the Author

Iris J Sarro, Ph.D is a daughter, wife, mother, grandmother, and friend. She is a widow living in Tampa with the blessings of family and friends. She is a school psychologist with more than a 45-year career dealing with the intricacies of relationships among parents, teachers, friends and others in the sphere of the student. The author was a staff school psychologist in one of the largest school districts in the US while completing her doctoral program at USF. She has trained many school psychology interns who have contributed much to the field and the students they have served. Her life journey includes balancing personal and professional relationships. coupled with lessons from her husband about living in the present moment. Life-long personal and professional relationships may be equally important to a satisfying life. The extent to which an individual lives in the present impacts the balance of these relationships. To live in the present and benefit from the past and not be afraid of the future can lead to healthy, satisfying relationships both personally and professionally, but it is more easily said than done!!

Dr Sarro has a private practice as a school psychologist who actively provides support to students, parents, and teachers. Professional experiences have taught Dr. Sarro that test results and grades are not the best measure of learning. Responding to the daily problems and challenges of life both inside and outside of the school setting are the greatest measure of learning. In reality the life experience is the greatest classroom. Dr. Sarro has authored a book on divorce and its impact on learning. Her work involves comprehensive evaluations that lead to interventions to improve the quality of the life of her students. If the student needs accommodations that qualify for a 504 Plan, or an Individualized Educational Plan (IEP), Dr. Sarro assists parents and teachers in writing those accommodations. She then provides on going consultation to implement and/or revise the accommodations as needed and actively provides support to students, parents, and teachers. The implementation of accommodations is what leads to improved quality of life for the student. It is rewarding to see students become self-advocates for themselves and enjoy more satisfying relationships at home and at school. In so doing Dr. Sarro often develops a life-long relationship with her clients that enable them to realize their potential and Dr. Sarro to realize what she was here to do.